S0-BBD-391

elegies

Publication of this book was supported by a
grant from the Eric Mathieu King Fund
of The Academy of American Poets.

Translation © 1996 by Keith Waldrop
This translation is published by arrangement
with Editions Gallimard, Paris, © 1967.

Some sections of this translation have appeared in Grosseteste, The
Literary Review, notus: new writing, o·blēk, *and* Scripsi.

Cover photograph is by Edward Holgate, from Stone Angels *series,
gelatin silver print, 1985.*

*This book was funded in part by a gift from Gail Sher and Brendan
Collins.*

ISBN 0-945926-44-8

jean grosjean

elegies

translated by keith waldrop

paradigm press
providence

I

A RUSTLING GAVE PROMISE you would turn your eyes towards me, while your hand was no more than bindweed along the hedge and, though winds may scatter my voice on the sterile sea like ashes from a fire, still I will have sung their birth.

For words you had only those green affirmations with their consonants, whose shape of fear on your mouth I so admire, your face trembling faintly in the dark fringe of your lashes.

Bees, blue sky, currants, poppies consort unceremoniously in your appearance, but your soul is woven from such deep winter that embers glow in my night and a nimbus rests on my spring, now that there is your pallor.

A bird singing above your snows would less have astonished me than the hue of storm with which your wide eyes flooded the sky at high tide, while my island foamed like a reef.

O promise, like that of orchards in April before lightning and hail assault them, I foresaw your antiquated tomorrows on a beach where waves, retiring, left lakes of sunlight on the sand.

The house where grapevines cling to rock did not imagine itself crumbling, but we know how summer uncrowns corymbs and how night batters our refuge with precious stones, before dawn's sentence breathes its last.

You in whose vulnerability I recognized my stock more than in dead certainties, in your eyes I have seen the momentary flicker and ineffable snuffing of the god we shudder to know or not to know.

Your name is the tree under which I sought shade and, when your hair came unbound in torrents, no autumn with bloodless foliage could have exhaled such imponderable vapors.

And what hoarfrost of the frontier was purer, what heartbeat skipped more at the gates of Chalindrey, than the kiss of our lips in greeting, while October's dead leaves spread flames across dark falling rivers?

No country bell on Sunday, no vine-stock purple with liquor, have bid the living to pomps like these, but I could never, without trembling, make plain the glories of which you are the temple, you are the season.

When the moon inclined between elms to examine the dew under your eyelids, I learned to go along only with you, unhurrying, towards funeral chambers lit by the flicker of your night-light.

If we climb again through stripped vines towards a springtime limpid with neither flowers nor sky, will you remember the hours we once lavished on roads, sure that the old deceiver beauty could only do us in?

Lucky for me that I watched for you to pass, since in this fog barred by dead trees the stars are no longer in their courses, as a flash of iron tread obliterates in the mud the prints of veined leaves and of boars.

II

WAS YOUR NAME NOT GIVEN me in prophecy before all things began, while my soul, deafened by silence, tottered on the rim of the well of heaven?

And when wild carnival music shook the clematis, I was certain you could stand up to the ruling angel's torrential nights.

But did you need so many and such long days to supplant our wars, our weeping, my thirst, and your own image in my heart—while signs and cyclones whirled about me?

Spring, on wan feet, walked lightly over the lake and away, periwinkle held in the teeth, to die of disgust in a thicket and leave no impression in the moss, for having failed to lie at length against your body.

Beset by such suns and so many stinging flies under the stifling foliage, by night I fled to sea to escape the buzzing that hindered me from hearing you breathe.

I have lain in wait for your voice in foreign syllables like rain unending on empty silos, finding respite only in the grassy ruminations with which I beguiled, languidly, my watch.

How may frenzies, their force spent, have left me stunned and shaking on a heap of demolished worlds, my cheek— across the storm—not touching your shoulder.

Oh yes, after your hard cautions and the sweet crimes by which I laid my ways open, how staggering to think I was hearing your approach, hearing your gaze from the verge of your lashes!

Solemnity, solemn rending of the veil when at three o'clock the god of doddering summers sees from an October threshold a nacreous sky within reach.

Then a bush burns by itself, all afternoon, far into a desert, with the crackling of your brief, half-spoken words — and no fork in the road could direct me to listen for others.

If some evening your ashes find rest in a gutter where a mild breeze mixes them with mine, can we know yet how high in the night the sparks from our fire will fly?

III

BLESSED NIGHT, WHEN THE Great Bear trembled beneath inverted peaks in a canal, while through your whispers I listened for my fever to lift.

Shadows were never more capacious than at the hour I heard my soul desert me with your footsteps, whose diminishing echo came back through the streets of a ghost town to beat at my heart.

Did you betray the solar plains of June and their sky tufted with cornflowers above the belfries, the night you lit—among blind houses—the great white bonfire of a sleepless dawn?

How, against a cliff scourged by sickly fruit and emaciated leaves, could I not thrill to this luster by which you contrived to cover my abysses with silence?

No cloud, nor buzzard, not a calyx dared sail on, when autumn stopped in the plummet of its decline, amid its spoils decked out to smile at you with lips of gold.

One evening, alas! winds and wolves in a pack heaved their sacrificial cries so high that I had to make off with you, across glittering spill from December candelabra.

But we recovered, over the yellow spume of recent snow and under sudden squalls of rain, the irrepressible idleness of late fall reflected on your brow and on your hips.

Acres of smoke pour up from burning stubble when, at the ditch the fugitives occupied, you lower your head and your hair comes unbound.

I have always cherished the rank weeds haunted by your wind-bitten ankles as we range a universe dismissed by your beauty, more serious than fatherlands.

Nothing extends or diminishes for long the minute space where, by turns, there reek about us the last teasel and the beginnings of decay.

Will our sleep, so long postponed by fall, hear in dreams the dropping apples or quails flying that we gave as pretext for our love,

or the opening rose or plum blossom, the maple or the briar stripped, leaves and sparrows and daylight in concerted farewell—at whose glory in your eyes I marvelled?

IV

NOW THAT THE BURDEN of its coruscating fruit blends the day into shadow, think how at the foot of motionless Julys you left the glaring dust of highways to let foxglove graze your back.

Once clear of the vast empty summer, its quivering edges quiet, you stretched, in the lean aftercrop on the gentle decline of age, your bare legs.

What did we know of joy, while the sun rolled childish and cruel over mountains we were scouring, amid haze from springs, for pale reflections of a today that was yet to come?

Already we plummet down the slant rain, along with red leaves and overripe fruit, to the ruts that lead back to their stable the oxen slavering silver on your hands.

Calm in the eye of storms is the farm where our yesterdays bleat in a half-light while unhitched clothing reeks at the blazing hearth, bringing the blood to your lips.

If the blue, slashed by winds, were to founder in clouds—its sparwork of branches leaving on the prairie spume nothing but straw snatched from hasty ricks—the sky remains unconquerable in your eyes.

Steam trickles down windows where birds press in vain to glimpse before dying the circles in which your eyes lift on me, in flashes, a cyanide clarity like the birth of archangels.

Hear how the hunters' guns reply weakly, from the trough of a downpour, to the crackling of our timbers when, rocked on the current of your hair, my sleep sinks downward towards your soul.

Never was nor ever will be dreamt more light than our hands held or more space than our footsteps opened as we walked into that shadow where your shadow is my wound and is my balm.

Stirrups, helmets, and regimental braid shine scattered on bedroom floors, like tears from lidless eyes in a face which, entombed, would not know if you beheld it.

V

SEPTEMBER COMES TO DWELL in us timidly, as a lamp in the dusk watches a wardrobe open onto dark flickerings and the garden draw to a close on your blush when you should not have come again.

Under what bleak spring's dead tree did I forget my name, running to see my dreams bed down in the sea when I had only moments more to wait for you?

My delirium drifted with the current towards hidden reefs until you vanquished the forces of hope with your mocking doubts.

And unexpectedly, for dawn's utmost miracle, with a long pensive sigh to stumble onto (as onto some hoofmark under the dew in an impenetrable clearing) your footprint between two lady's-slippers!

What wonderful portents I've seen under dead brush and in clouds just before nightfall, when—like a lovely stretching forth of shadows—your hand reached me, absolving you of their promises.

The man who climbed a budding slope to contemplate from afar the rose plains came back again along dark pools, smitten only by sadness, without an inkling that your star would rise above the woods.

The pale mist that covers streams when the moon strikes its flint against their banks—my wild heart trusted it less than your soul, which veils your body without hiding it.

From the gloomy orchard where your burdens of scent are stored, mounts with its soft rustle of flags your passionately slow flame.

Even if thrones and shrines and the constellations should challenge you with their gems, nothing can undo that in our passing hour a leaf falling into shadow dilated no iris but yours.

VI

AROUND THE HOUSE the night rain circles on the grass with light steps like your steps in memory of which my lashes will be wet still under the ground.

The light of dawn, over standing pools that it illuminates amid patient drip from the ashtrees, comes to beleaguer your chamber with a silence which says our day is waiting for you.

The shadow of the sparrow-hawk barely grazes dead leaves strewn as you make your way towards the ruined sanctuary, not so much as raising an eyebrow.

Rushing waters, if the rains resume, will halt you only at a cliff's edge where it will be up to me, letting go of your fingers, to descend with the salt of your tears as viaticum.

All our shattered hours will have been a single instant of sunlit wine-harvest before in drunkenness our scrambled names roll harborless at the mercy of seaswell.

Joy was unforeseeable and raging winds failed to rend it and neither will our shrouds muffle it.

However husks may dessicate under matting and timid suns drop their silk-work of gossamer on the stubble, your eyes remain act of seeing and your hands of gesture.

I live since I have known your laughter, and the nettles in their spring will never choke out the print of your foot.

Some evening, may you quit like autumn mist the roof under which we supped on curds, and together we will prowl along the border of the final snows.

Don't you hear in the distance the horsemen falling back in disorder into death, which they spatter with smutty oaths as their empire gives way to our winter?

VII

FROM THE HIGHEST POINT of the longest night, the moon floods the room where I keep you watching for the coming of the Month of Snows with its rimy teeth and its pure cry of a stray hoot-owl.

Our own azure was sick from thinking of those grand rays whose dialogue thronged original darkness, inconsolable save by the night's return.

Will we lose track now of the pallid hours when crimson suffused both the leaves and your cheeks which faced the dew that dawn had distilled by way of enigma or of promise?

More follies have entered your eyes than were ventured in the sky by the seasons with their whirlwinds, their bows, their flares, or their breath misting the back of your neck.

The flowering cherry, breathing under stormclouds the black odor of the soil, was ruined as quickly as (out our window, not distracting me from you) a summer's day over the still forest.

We come back from life as, children, we returned from school, along a path strewn with gold by an October evening, marvelling to have learned which words contain the world.

Nothing lied and, if the shadow little by little did wear away your glorious face, the fragrance of your head on my shoulder is more tenacious than your smile was.

Oh yes, a wind mews treacherous under the door and death down in the courtyard barks at a fallen leaf rearing, but your unrepentant road was such that, dead, I'll have your name to murmur.

Won't a chip of rock, a drop of water, a fragment of star sunk in an old pond or the wing of an insect lost in the grass persist in repeating in their night the bright ray that glanced them?

VIII

FOR WHAT DO YOU KEEP vigil standing in the fog with the dark battalions of pine, unable to tell earth from sky?

The day's obscurity weighs so that only night could bring relief, were it not for the long and indecipherable gaze with which you hold our enemies in check.

Leave the hedges their blur of dog-rose and their shadow against the sky, but keep your doubts for me or else take mine.

Tear me from my life and from the dead in a lambent flight on feathered wings and make me a prey to your elevation.

I hear my soul rasp at your approach, your step like pale stars walking on haze.

Delivered from my liberty, I wed in you dear Poverty, her empty hands more beautiful than diamonds of the Indies.

May I, the eve of my agony, sleep on a hillside, trembling till I wake wrapped in dew by your breath.

IX

MY SOUL WOULD FAST DISSOLVE in shadow if you followed the spot of sunlight which turns a few hours across ivy or moss to remain only a memory that night mistrusts.

Do not withdraw from me as did the grand sad palmy days of childhood with their heavenly corollas at the ankles and their blue abysses overhead.

What does it matter that my mornings have shrunk back into the pungent boxwood or bursting gillyflowers if you reign in their stead without interregnum.

Would you slip away by paths of fragile mayflowers where the angelus expires along silky catkins weeping because of a cuckoo's call?

Think of the shoreless dereliction to which I was consigned one evening by the poplars while night submerged breeze and crows in a nest of trembling stars.

Impossible, intolerable, untrue—that you could be simply the image of what you were and elude my living death behind the unalterable impression of your face.

Why be jealous of fall's royal unconcern which along with its ungathered grapes, its brazen walnuts, its gold dust in suspense, it deposits on the thresholds it deserts?

You will speak to me again, if only by the lightest flutter of your lashes, or at least you will hear me utter from the depth of my soul your name, nothing but your name, with fearful effort and hollow voice raised from the pit.

Time that carries in its windings tool-handles and happy-new-year mistletoe has for a long time, on the parapet, let me offer only to you—who offer only to me—the little water human hands can hold.

The day in decline throws eastward the shadow of the gesture that we will continue through the night to claim from the immortals when the springs of the worlds have all gone dry.

X

I HARDLY NOTICED A GLOSSY great bird asleep in the moonlight the night I ran to meet you.

How often I've passed the crack of dusk or dawn without knowing—sapphire and shadow of the sky so confounded, and nightingales with the groaning storm—if we turned back or hurried down the hours,

without foreseeing how disheveled chrysanthemums would shine through the fog in triumph or in fever, without bringing to mind caparisoned horses that trampled August roses drawing the coffin I had escaped.

Now, behind disinherited forests crossed by the last migrating cranes, evening smoulders on the verge of a winter almost as near and as nude as you.

Already our house mixes into shadows its tiles and the white smoke from its hearth, in front of which your dreams caress your body with invisible shudders.

Odor of dead branches and of apples permeates the vast room and also your hair, whose silhouette along your hip shines silkier and more saluted than the colors of the Guard.

Neither footpaths filled with musing butterflies nor versicles streaking the page with responses have come to any clarity purer than that which shelters under your lowered lashes.

How better extol your burning lips than by lifting to them a taste of cold beer in this old bowl, battered as the walls of Jericho?

The wardrobe with sporadic creaking supplants the embers whose holy sighs are stifled in the windings of your ear.

Soon day will advance among the branches, displaying a sky as virginal as your teeth when you prepare to say my name.

XI

IF I WERE GOD I WOULD have had fingers only for fashioning in the soul your face, of which your body is the incorruptible aura and the universes only a shadow.

Let November immerse in its mists crumbling walls and roads from the lowlands to allow your gathering from the dead tree the great red fruit of autumn's end.

One day again we've been together, or hardly a day, time hurried so, but in the dark I will devour its sun on your mouth.

Your eyes closed their flower behind them, in order to brighten the shadow I will be plunged into by hours that no longer see you.

If you fall asleep in the sepulchres of the world, I will despise the *luceat eis quam olim Abrahae promisisti et semini ejus.*

I will watch from an extinguished planet the human earth gleam murmuring from afar, like an urban cemetery on Sunday, full of the living who have not known your name.

But if your soul fell silent within my soul, farewell! we would not even have existed, nothing, no one, with God no doubt left dreaming himself alone.

In vain would stardust have sparkled in pools on your pathway or resin tears on your eyelids if I had not seen them.

Space was merely the distance and our hour merely the time it took for you to see yourself in my words and for me to hear my voice on your face.

XII

See the meagre vapor my cry released when evening followed so close on dawn, no time for springs to drink in passing clarities.

Now I am dead or close to it but no lambency reaches me from the grave, where I had hoped to see blazing the runes that you recite.

Where trails descend and the steel-surfaced river, you are left on the peak, its bones bared by lightning.

I know your light stays on but when my eyes go out will I have harbored only a dreadful thirst?

Was that why you woke me, so that going back to sleep I remember you—and the night, dreaming of you, is different?

But you, what would you remember, unless you live in the faint underground clamor that succeeds your voice?

Give me again a poplar grove, its gold tinkling with each breath of fall under the soft sky, where the wild cherry tree laves impalpable waves over its lean reddened limbs.

May my soul in its sepulchre still shine from your beauty that I have seen face to face.

When the last drum beats reveille you will behold in my eyes of a tyro the lines erased that will have razed your cheek.

XIII

IF THE HELLEBORE OPENING its greenish flower does not bend our eyes towards a winter thicket, it is because your face is our hearts' fascination.

Your light shines nearer on a humid outcrop of rock and more limpid in the bare tree than could summers of heaven with their interminable suns.

While you are obscured by clouds flinging wool and arrows against the hills, the few flakes of snow they drop into our furrows shine farther in the depths of evening than geraniums in Berlin.

Rising, you raised eyes that day whose shadow now falls on us and your pallor is the last sign my eyes serve, while victories twist their lips in rage.

Where are the wars for which you were the trophy, now that a single cannon in the distance thunders as occasionally as a yawn and hope weeps among consuls crunching birds' bones?

Have your sentences, whose shadow and portent long turned seaward, foundered—leaving the space of the world but a desert between us?

The more I bury myself in the country to escape the tides rehashing their inept sermon with a mouthful of pebbles, the louder I hear the breakers of your silence.

The leaves you were losing adore—prostrate on the ground—your naked gesture they had concealed, or else lift in the wind to graze your fingers still raised to me.

Supposing the sun withdrawn into shadow as quietly as your hands, in order to hear—adoring in the dark—your voice which I heard hush, in the ground I will distinguish the shadow in which I left your body when I chose your soul as my lamp.

Since our dark is without stars and our days sunless, I hate dawns that would dare leave in the dew prints not of your foot.

Creak as it did, that long hearse that carried you, each day I search under dead brambles its wondrous wheelruts where at Easter sprang up comfrey.

XIV

LIFT YOUR HEAD INTO THE WIND until your hair sprays against my face, like a dark All Hallows thundercloud, its whispering fragrance.

Oh never—unless protected by ancient ritual, like a priest or like the river Meuse—bend above the blue or yellow lichen that, a millennium, dreamt of seeing your bosom fill with breath.

So slowly your eyes or your hips swing round to prayer that air goes muttering through bushes the Month of Sleet, a sluice-gate lifting to freshets.

Your eyelids ever so slightly lift and I'm in a light like that the seven heavens, cleft by the angel, will scatter.

When you would take the wooded path for nothing more than its daylight and its tomtits, I hear your footsteps in the coppery leaves that step by step kiss your heel and die at length of your reflection.

Our breathless phrases once blown out, only owls make response from one or another tree, but the evening is musky for a moment above the stump you'll no longer be sitting on.

The moon, perched on a branch, in vain counts out to you graves among the yews—you knew how hasty men are, except for one in love with you.

A dawn unsealing your leaded eyes, you would see how in memory of you the hoarfrost embellishes our dump.

Fearing a warm fruit might still sleep beneath fresh snows, the dead will hesitate to trample territory you have haunted.

XV

PAST THE TOWN, its glossy eyes staring through fog, we had no sun but the big dishevelled nest hanging from the branches.

Cold wrapped you in its coat as you strode across silly frontiers, regardless of assaults to come.

Storms nonetheless shed no scorn—from their shaky hands, their branching arms—on your pain-marked skin or the veined iris of your eyes.

Now that it's winter I live in your wood-locked house of torment where evenings we go out along the hedges and invoke the glimmer that keeps vigil atop a holly.

Should a war extinguish every lamp in the world, in the dark I shall hear all the better those words you withheld while robins went swaggering among the box.

Do I need eyes to see you lift your eyes from a pit into which you have fallen towards the inaccessible heights where you would be no longer prey?

Were your feet already at the zenith and my temples still buried beneath the clay, I would catch your name before mine but you would know better than your own my heart amid its brambles.

I never hoped to understand myself, only—you seeing me—
to watch you suffer our worlds, your soul unclouded.

In what opaque depths do straying suns burn out in haggard
fires, troubling you less than my death?

XVI

Rain whipping my face or soul sunk into fever, I find your peace in the gale, your sky in the shadows, your shadow in the gutter.

I have found your well-head only in deserts, surprised your heart only in that silence whose abyss I plowed—but your beauty enthralls me in the horrors of your fatherland.

Ah, my old-time trudge through storms, amid slush for the feet to slide in, the only dim lamp in my soul your eyes' intermittent glimmer like waves of steel in northern seas.

Your footsteps above the dead sing in November of a miry earth haunted by glaucous sky and your shoulders dignify those whimpering willows lost in a bend of the dell.

Gusts over the fen that make me cringe whirl leaves away with my dreams, no more able to tear you from those dreams than to divide the veins of a leaf from the leaf.

Gloom of days pierced by erring flames from the pupils of one-eyed beasts, as still-born dawn creeps up the horizon, proving no hindrance to my hearing your hush!

If I did not live in the echo of your silence, I would be like men, those straws the raven weaves into his throne on the branch.

Since no one has slaked my thirst, it remains for the light of your lips soon to reopen the tremulous primrose and perhaps my eyes.

XVII

WITHOUT PHANTASMAGORIA, without your face after face, without your face but without hiding your eyes or at least the soul in your eyes, you come to a standstill on the paling grass and in gum arabic fires.

Always there's night and its morning to recognize it, like a runaway horse nosing out an old cart behind the barn and I don't know what to do, what to run from.

Could I, in a room where you would not be, live between my late body and my soul gone mad, under the corpse's horrible fixed stare, amid howls of expectation?

But I endure the increasing light, like that from your scent in the dark when I renounced all your seemings, studying to admit only you.

I was perishing in the whining storm that filled the village, when suddenly I glimpsed your suffocating glow behind the bushes on the hillside.

Done with, fleeting promises or appalling vague vainglories, if now I see you in your eyes.

The sky's coarse brocade is torn on the dead junk-littered grass where you stand like a winter tree, your soul unmasked.

I recognize my heart in your anguish, my sickness in your agony and your triumph of loss.

Your soul is the soul's sleeplessness, a prowling wind ridden with doves snatching straws of gold from rotting haystacks, their eyes bloodshot.

XVIII

UNDER DARK RENTS in the rainy sky, I press windward towards your day's end struggling on a western hill.

Dearer for being half mired, your evening in the heart of the vineyard wrings its hands over a hoard of glimmers ashen and rose.

Did your light slip under the horizon faster than my knees into the thickets when I feared you might, alas, turn away?

So the blind man, anguished, retraces—hardly disturbing the sleeping birds—your dark path, the scent of your passage.

May I find again at the center of the dark, in the forest from which you hastened at dawn, your house falling to mildew.

By feeling out the trees from whose arms balls of mistletoe tremble, I will find in the dark your door that, leaving, you could not close.

As soon as squalls subside, I divine in the hum of failing worlds a thud of humus your gesture would make.

At ground's end a yellowish slit opens to confirm my perdition, while all I dreamt was of your night.

Why were you there, what muted profile will you venture into the false light, dawning without power to hide from me your sullen lips?

XIX

RENDING THE VEIL which concealed the dark, you only cast a light into the void, where your steps rustle the branches and your fingers stroke sparks from linen.

You were just your own transience in which I could find rooms more vacant than my own uninhabitable lodgings under runnels of singing rain.

Stray scents of hay, of rancid snacks, of wet fox fur—they speak of you, like a buzz of prophecies crouched in the thickets.

The farther I wander off, the more I sense you around me, in your scattered traces, the vapor above the woods, a bird's flight, the chink of some stone.

I'm forever running to places you've just left, without sight of you either on my tracks or in my heart, as you laugh in silence as the gods laugh.

You stand alert in my memory and thwart my attempts to hem you in, you who can assume a vacant gaze in which the reeds blend into the fog.

The jolting of a wagon at peep of day or of a winter sun over the hills—your excuses to obsess my heart like the muffled beat of animals in the barn or a knell overhead.

Obliterate your name if you will, you cannot turn me from you, you bound by nothing, from whom I am unbound neither by sleep nor by joy nor by death.

I am prey to your ancient catastrophe, with its uncertain clarities, its lost intonations, and that flavor of first violets munched at daybreak of the resurrection.

XX

Do YOU KNOW HOW sick and tired I am of trembling by the puddles or about the grass you cross, never running to meet you along with brisk rains?

Your name so weighs on me, its band pressed into my skin, that I manage no works, no dreams, not even betrayal.

How to follow you over the rough ground or leave you, I your shadow, as you walk into the rising sun?

Recumbent in the bed of rubble where spiders tread lightly, I admire your step which puffs me up, and I deface it.

Deliver me not to wild animals, do not loose your foot from mine and—if the day rise higher than your height—be yet the blind for my dusk.

When you sit with your eyes of blue sky over the mountain, my strength scatters out among brome grass and cow dung.

I alone have known how under your silken flesh your bones are rock crystal, but between red petals, beneath your wounds, I will see your soul passing.

If you behold in me your own abyss, let me find breath again in your odor of resin and ash.

XXI

SEE THE RAVENS, like my thoughts, wheel above the clearings where widows gather dead wood for a last fire.

Do you come from a town where, day and night, angels sparkle in windows under which glide mutterings or haze from streets and canals?

Sometimes summer closes its shutters caressed by the sun, till the hour for the moon to sigh over a plane tree less somber than my heart when you've forgotten.

You know how it sleeps in the dawning light, the citadel a dying man quits for your stretches of desert—where you fashion my space.

Tonight in your wide eyes I see, above the woods, the falling flakes of white which obliterate our pathways faster than the dark.

No one but you could have laid siege to me with these soughing village fumes in the dead of winter.

I will lie down among the illustrious dead in the ice where your soul has already mirrored its face of crevices.

Nothing now will keep you from hearing far off the breaking tides or, at your doorstep, the thin Arabian snow melting.

XXII

IF I FORGET YOU, you prowl windows with the livid purple and blue acid that stars cast onto gelid boughs in the dead orchard.

You've only to skim with a glance the world's frost, and the dark floes are to me fire of azure and of roses.

With no more eloquence than a shrug of your shoulders you break out day in the branches and in my heart under the snow.

I wanted only you without knowing you and betrayed only you without naming you, since the first leaf, sprung from the first blind bud, warped and crumpled, remembered its forms to come.

Are you aware that if you had not in your labors blundered within our four walls, I would have died here at the window waiting for you?

A curse on what's left of the brambles for not one of them that evening catching your leg, to make blossom there the streaks of blood your mouth contemplates.

Between your lashes pass slowly, endlessly, the low thunderclouds which come from leaden seas with their luminescent shadows to frame my days with your eyes.

Do not be astonished that from a lopped road an abrupt wind of joy arises—less forceful, to be sure, than your glance.

The burning bark, under drizzles that unsnow our land, lights up your face between columns of smoke whose incense my words send up to you.

How blessed, along the midden of centuries, the hour I consume in puzzling out your soul, and that kiss of your glory on my eyes.

XXIII

WE HEARD CROWS IN the thunderheads crying their home-
less cries while the soul thought to leave your body.

Will you, if the meadows turn green again, leave your hair
thread by thread to the sparrows who hang their retreats in
the rushes?

But you are worth more than incorruptible gold, you whose
blood flows noiselessly beneath your skin towards an estu-
ary dredged twice daily by death's dark tides.

I've no longer anything to say except to you, since your
glory is unveiled but lightless and nearly faceless or of a
beauty only divined in the shadows.

You were silent enough for me to understand what promise
you would keep, when my life—born from knowing you—
could no longer die.

Even if you are no longer visible to the eyes, I will see you,
but the blind who walk the earth shall grasp only our
clothes.

Under the somber heavens challenged by your gaze, our
abode holds its own against the gods' encampment, whose
border limits our horizons.

Rain crossing the garden encounters skeletons who next summer will hold to your maybe widowed mouth a green-gage.

Will you hear for long the musicians I paid to magnify your mourning, the mould devouring my lips unable to stop my heart from calling your name?

XXIV

YOU SLEEP WITH THE FOG against the bare earth warmed only by your blood that within myself I hear feebly beating.

If the masters who don't know you, were to instruct me, I would hear beneath their balanced syllables your breath breathe lightly over humid moss.

Old comrades may well laugh, hands pressed to war wounds, but nothing prevents my descent to your spring lit by a lichen-covered tree.

No, do not wake, do not tell me that you wake, do not tell me that we wake when you know we are dreaming.

Shadow this universe is, full of ghost towns and deserts under construction, with its ocean lungs and its starry tops spinning in your hair.

Our words we hear only in dreams, without our speaking, not whipping your heart with those long love lines whose backlash would bloody my soul.

A marvelous appearance still hides your true beauty that we will die of once our souls embrace body to body.

Patience, let us sleep like the text in the book, like the body in the grave, until the moment I can abide you and have no more need for worlds.

The hideous pain, as long as men and days keep moving on the earth, is nothing beside the joy that will kill us when we come alive.

Be quiet, let me swallow my saliva, turn my eyes away for a moment, crush out the still smoking sun, and I'll be ready to have time no more for hope or fear.

XXV

WHERE WERE YOU WHEN the mercenaries said to me, Let's sack the villages, and the afternoon swung across me the shadow of a bored yew?

What were you waiting for at the end of a winter when the snow hung on in the woods behind which I felt my fear drift?

I learned despair against a bare wall, watching harvest fields quiver with poppies you never saw.

And who would come to drive away the wasps from a trellis where clusters of grapes turned purple outside your ken?

No one, except perhaps a dead man, will ever find again, in the depths of time gone by, the locales where you stood me up.

But will we lose all trace of those hours whose embers were your voice and of which your body will be merest ash?

Enough that your limbs move through the grass for centaury to blossom or the sun to lean down and drink from the spring.

Weeks became nothing but your face turning towards me torn light and torn night.

How do so many slow years slip by leaving me only memory, as dreadful as your heart?

But our day, which was every day new, cannot end even if the hoarse blackbird should intone our graves under the rain.

XXVI

BETTER SPITE FROM YOU than silence if you leave me with this sham life stirred, evenings, by men working the road.

What I've suffered from the derisive stars, while dawn with its green glances could never distinguish you in the brake!

For a long time now your name has been only the whisper of a breeze prowling the leaves, but my heart has heard nothing else.

Since your face is the site of my soul I would prefer hate from you to contempt, but don't pay too much attention to what I say.

I admit I've preferred your contempt to wandering by fog-bound pools, unsure if you hid in the tall reeds.

How, after you looked on me, could I traverse again the desert days when you were neither sun nor shadow?

I swore to you that you need not be ashamed of my downward path towards night, but if I am forsworn do not alarm yourself.

So many dead leaves rotting away in ponds in honor of spring, I will increase your glory in my downfalls.

The dusk or dawn sky is white in the bright November or April tree but it is always the season to present you with my earliest soul or my last.

XXVII

WHAT RAPIER DIVIDES my soul, opens at the center of my heart this void of being separated from you and how you die of mourning and how I am dying?

The flesh of roses rots and water grows stagnant in ponds but I think I know hatred.

Uhlans and famine and death trample this path where you will weep for our day with its head already bowed above the cemetery hills.

Were you not my protracted light on the summer evening when, overcome by love, I sank into a dream obsessed by stars?

When your trembling approach woke me before cockcrow, did I unseal my eyes then only to sleep again to be born?

Destruction profanes us and its Prince walks on our eyes but his demons scrape in vain at the memory inside my skull where your name is not liable to disappear.

From what pit was the world delivered of so many subterranean gods with faces of carbon and torture tongs—unable to keep your phosphorescent bones from floating through my night?

Yes I hush, but dregs of my words among the aspen tips still murmur your soul which they concealed.

XXVIII

On the leaves the fog plants drop by drop its scattered footsteps, all the more weird as your beauty remains veiled.

The sky, riddled with branches and colorless, rests on the roof, transmitting from time to time a rook's cry, all the more insolent as you are silent.

Amnesiac in the retreating day, I lower my troubled gaze to the mirror where my breath mists your image.

When widowed carillons ring to wake our ruins in the waste places, will I see you again, across the thickets, remerging your way with mine?

I'll grasp again the hope of seeing your eyes as they lit our first encounter and running to meet we will bruise the kindred grass.

What did we forget in sleep that we must again, one Sunday morning, slip across the breezes that separate us and that uncover you?

From far off, I caught the throb of your birthday party, saw only its fading reflection all evening along the vineyard, where the flowering peaches understood my pain!

I knew you were gone, by stars wheeling above the desert until dawn whose long shadows crept with the scorpions back under the rocks.

Neither the lightning that whipped night seas under a coast-line bathed in tears nor purplish cockleburs, looking sickly amid the wheat, have disappointed your hour.

Now you can be quiet as an inner chamber or murmur with white willows the simple words we thought too much on under the headstone of the dark.

My time snapped up in the abyss and my body half stoned by materials, I shelter my face in the flash of your eyes.

How many forlorn battles I've deserted for these junipers where our rendezvous is my revenge on the devil and on your grave.

XXIX

COMPLICITY OF UNPOLISHED stones on the ground with the gleam of your breath-filled flesh, my heart's opaque flame tuned to your translucent shadow.

A purer light is born in your eyes with the decline of the season whose fevered leaves, mingled with feathers, fall on the shore.

Your deeper fierier voice forecasts how death in turn will fall exhausted in our bodies where death's night thinks to win.

As a horse that sniffs dust averts his nostrils, should I linger in suburbs you no longer inhabit?

The blue sky, its cohorts broken by storm, comes back in homage to your lips, your eyelids—that we had supposed dispersed in the grave.

I must, unawares, have picked this day when I first glimpsed your soul.

Each hour spreads its snow corolla that my breath strews on the water and whose fruit your mouth will ripen.

At what moment can I pull away from you without falling as cinders into spaces that have no ground unless you stretch out your hand?

Pyrites at rest in the trough of the sea and the ammonite in its mountainside are sentences of yours gone to sleep—that I dread and hanker to rouse.

For your words astonish, like branches lost upside down in the sky, and in haste at the watering place I gather up forgotten stars to answer you.

XXX

HOW COULD IT BE already dully bright behind the trees and on the water in the trench, when we have slept only a single hour?

The rain of early-falling nights quenched our kerosene suns and you declined behind walls.

Then the blind storms sang to lull my anger and I resisted them no longer.

I was no longer anything but a clump of dead moments, a clod of cold sparks thrown after you into the pit.

But how brief a night eternal night since, losing my footing here, I find you again and the lark ascending sings her lungs out.

Your smile is still the same, with just that shadow of a wrinkle pain has left behind.

Though the iris of your eyes is deeper, I see your fire there smouldering under the waste.

Do not clutter with gestures your light, the marvel of pools, if you hear me above the murmur of leaves listening to you.

XXXI

IT WAS A LONG EVENING that forged our night, when you lit the lamp of the dead and your breath did not bend its flame.

When there was nothing more I could see but the terror in your dark-dilated eyes, were we not even then a thousand times repaid for being born?

Since you have known me from time's beginning, do not temper your charge against the shadows.

Let the city gates, where streets run out, lift their lintels onto a sky riddled with stars and tattered—less than you— by dawn.

I recall your head, on a level with the rising sun caught in the brambles like a fatted yellow lamb.

The leaves without blades and the leafless trees have crystal nerves which the calm light suffuses and an invisible bird scarcely chirps for fear of frightening you.

Did you think the waves would roll back, leaving us that shoreless moment, or that the woods would slough its shadow and—so abruptly—our bodies their demise?

Here we are then, swept by cold rains, dried in night winds where shadows flickered, glittering with frost and scars, with my eyes there to read your eyes.

XXXII

IN THE MOUNTAINS, on the bright budding tree, the blackbird unleashes his voice to glorify the sinuous line of your back.

If it rains as if smiling on the savage mind of the cemetery, your face shines more brightly than gravelly beaches burnished by our tides.

Shod by warm mists in the Month of Seed, I stub my clumsy toe on a blue pebble and the heavenly noise hurtles towards the abyss where we lived.

The warmth of life reascends our hearts as our ankles sink in snow thawing between anemones, or as your glance sweeps my forehead.

Already the violent blue of the heights rests on your back, as my hand used to rest on your shoulder which still trembles.

Conscious that you are preparing to interrogate, I drop my eyes to your cool legs behind which spread all the wooded hills of eastern Gaul.

Now that the sun is at your knees, the raven soaring slowly over the world lets his shadow stray only to your hip where, each eve of battle, my head has rolled.

Past horrid straits, I listen—in a complicitous and contagious light—to the faint rustle of your eyelids as they first lifted.

XXXIII

STEP BY STEP I ADVANCED into your glory, deep in autumn and age, amid squandered gold and the sound of leaves underfoot.

Too marvelous winter whose pure glimmer you became on my heavy eyelids! and I was seized by a terrible drowsiness while grass sprang reborn in the valley.

First visage and last clarity, nothing could wake me on the Alps except your look of fire, of snow, of soul.

Stretch out your hand to me, like an apple tree in a May orchard which we loved for its promise, and your lips like new wine.

I recapture in the scent of trailing ivy your dark armpit and my thirst for your eyes which unsteady the April sky.

For regalia you bear only marks from the muffled fight we fought against the angel of empire in his caverns.

This writing, which patiently and a long while called to me cryptically from the depth of my soul, lights your body.

This book was set in 10 point Century Schoolbook and was printed at McNaughton-Gunn, Saline, Mich.

The editor thanks the following patrons for their generous support of paradigm press:

Kristina Hamm
Donn & Temple Nelson
James & Marlene Frisbie
Victoria & Scott Frisbie
Claudia Fishman
Rachel & Jay Tarses
George Rattner
Ray & Frances Stark
Marilyn Netter
Gail Sher & Brendan Collins